The Tao of Red States and Blue States

The Tao of Red States and Blue States

Ed Bremson

iUniverse, Inc.
New York Lincoln Shanghai

The Tao of Red States and Blue States

iUniverse books may be ordered through booksellers or by contacting:

iUniverse
2021 Pine Lake Road, Suite 100
Lincoln, NE 68512
www.iuniverse.com
1-800-Authors (1-800-288-4677)

ISBN-13: 978-0-595-35967-7 (pbk)
ISBN-13: 978-0-595-80417-7 (ebk)
ISBN-10: 0-595-35967-1 (pbk)
ISBN-10: 0-595-80417-9 (ebk)

Printed in the United States of America

To my younger self, c. 1963:
Thank you.

You knew the correct path even then.
I found my way back.

Prologue

Everyone who watched TV or read the news during the last two Presidential elections has heard of Red States and Blue States. Basically the Red States were the ones won by George W. Bush, and the Blue States were those won by his opponents—Al Gore in 2000 and John Kerry in 2004.

Thinking about Red States and Blue States reminded me of Chinese Philosophy. As the reader may know, yin/yang is a concept that deals with opposites such as dark/light, female/male, night/day, etc. The Red States and Blue States have qualities that are antithetical to each other too. In this book we will examine some of those qualities, particularly as they relate to the teachings of the *Tao Te Ching*, a 2000 year-old Chinese manuscript of wisdom and advice.

The Tao of Red States and Blue States is not intended to be a scholarly work. It is more a work of art. It is also an opinion piece of sorts. In writing this book I relied on the knowledge and beliefs I acquired while following the news for the past several years. I also relied on my imagination and on a detailed reading of the *Tao Te Ching*.

The Tao of Red States and Blue States is not a theory of Politics. It is a theory of, or philosophy of a media image, of dynamics between the two major political parties, and of election results, all from a Taoist perspective. The focus, therefore, is quite specific.

I hope this book will stimulate the reader to think and to do research for himself. He may find it interesting to read the *Tao Te Ching* in conjunction with reading this text. Each passage in this book is essentially based on a passage in the *Tao Te Ching*. I have therefore numbered my passages to correspond with their numbered counterparts in the *Tao Te Ching*. The reader also may find it interesting to read the *Tao Te Ching* independently. I consulted the 1891 James Legge translation while writing this book, but there are many other translations available that are more modern and readable. Those of Stephen Mitchell and Ursula K. Le Guin come readily to mind.

Finally, I tried to be impartial while writing this book. I hope I succeeded.

There is nothing about its name that makes a state Red or Blue. There is nothing about its location or its climate or its pace of life. There is something about the hearts and minds of men and women, an appealing candidate with an agreeable message, whether the message appeals to the heart or to the mind or to both, or to something else unknown. All that and more makes a state Red or Blue. (1)

Knowing a Red State, we can easily imagine a Blue State. Knowing someone from a Red State, we can easily imagine someone from a Blue State. They don't value the same things we value. They don't believe the same things we believe. By and large, however, you can't tell a Red State person from a Blue State person just by looking at him or her. There is something inside, not outside, that makes a person Red or Blue.

Given the idea of Texas, we can easily imagine more Red States. Given the idea of Massachusetts, we can easily imagine more Blue States. The only problem is that often we deal in stereotypes in which everyone who votes Red lives in a certain area of the country, and everyone who votes Blue lives in a certain area of the country. But that's just not true. Some Blue voters live in Texas and some Red voters live in Massachusetts. (2)

In the exercise of Politics, the Reds seek to not excite the Blues, and the Blues seek to not excite the Reds. The more excited each side is, the more likely they are to vote. Neither side wants the other side to go out and vote. (3)

The idea of Red States and Blue States is a recent idea. As a concept, however, it is not new. Political divisions have always existed, just as yin and yang have always existed. In both cases, the concepts awaited the particular graphical representations that we see today: in the former case, a map of the United States with some States colored Red and some colored Blue; in the latter case, the familiar yin/yang symbol from Oriental art. Red States and Blue States are not as absolute, black and white, as are yin and yang, but they are just as evenly divided. (4)

Red States and Blue States
Could be compared to
The two sides of a bellows,
To two men arguing,
To two lovers loving,
Or to any number
Of pairs of opposites.
When one side
Interacts with the other side
Something is produced
Or destroyed.
That is the Way of the *Tao*.
Indeed, that is the Way of the world.
We don't always like what results from
This interaction of opposites.
That is particularly true
In politics.
But at least in
The Red States and Blue States
We must accept the results. (5)

Red States and Blue States could be compared to a father and a mother: when a man and a woman come together and make a child, one never knows beforehand what offspring will result. And though we are not always surprised by who is elected when the Red States and Blue States vote, we are usually surprised by the manner in which he is elected. (6)

The Red States and Blue States may continue for a long time, or not.

In some instances it is easier for a Blue State to become a Red State than vice versa.

Some States will always be Red. Some States will always be Blue. Some States may change from election to election. They are called Swing States. (7)

The *Tao Te Ching* says, "The excellence of a residence is in the suitability of the place." Red States are suitable in some ways, and Blue States are suitable in other ways. Red States are more suitable at certain times of the year, and Blue States are more suitable at other times of the year. Some States are more suitable for certain activities than other States. And each State has its own unique offerings of food. But in some instances, what one person finds suitable another person finds unsuitable. (8)

The Blue States say that Government can help solve many of our social problems.

The Red States say that Government is part of the problem.

Meanwhile the rich get richer and the poor get poorer. (9)

In ruling a State, there seems to be a choice between helping disadvantaged people or helping large corporations. And it seems that the Reds make the latter choice, whereas the Blues make the former. (10)

You can't have a Red State without Blue voters. It wouldn't make sense. A State is Red not because there were only Red votes, but because there were more Red votes than Blue votes. That's what Red means. Take away all the Blue voters and you might still have a Red State, in some sense, but not the same Red State. (11)

When we look at a Red State we see blue sky and green everywhere, but no red, except perhaps in the red of a flower, the sky at sunset, the colors of certain sports teams, etc. But the same is true of a Blue State: same red sky/blue sky that we find in a Red State. So it's not the sky that makes a State Red or Blue. It is an election. (14)

When we look at a State, we may ask ourselves, "Where is the Redness that makes that State Red? Where is the Blueness that makes that State Blue?"

As hard as we look, we will never see those qualities with our eyes, for they are in the hearts and minds of the people who live there and vote. (14)

It is not enough for a candidate to craft a message that appeals to his constituency of Red or Blue. He must craft a message that motivates his constituency to actually vote. A State can become Red, for example, by an absence of Blue voters, as well as by an abundance of Red voters. Turnout is key.

And some may say, isn't a candidate who "crafts his message" being phony and not genuine? These days, with focus groups and pinpoint polling, a candidate must craft his message. Either that or lose. (15)

People vote for candidates they like and trust, and with whom they can identify. We have all seen men lose elections because they seemed out of touch with regular people. If you want to win a Red State, then Red State voters must like you, and you must appear to like them, perhaps to the point of being one of them.

It's not the same with Blue States. Just look at Al Gore and John Kerry. With all the baggage that those two had, the Blue States voted for them anyway, and they came within a hair of winning it all. So the Blue States are looking for something different in a candidate than are the Red States. It therefore seems that if you had a Blue candidate who somehow appealed to Red voters, he would automatically win all the Blue States, some of the Red States (one or two might be enough) and thereby the election. Does John Edwards fit this scenario? Wesley Clark? (15)

The time between Presidential elections is a time of relative stillness, at least on the surface. In reality there is a great deal of activity. Some of the activity begins when the last election ends. Much of it begins at least several years before the next election. During that in between time, a State that was Red still has the potential to become Blue, and a State that was Blue has the potential to become Red. Some States have a higher probability of making that change than do others. (16)

Some voters are swayed by lies while some voters are not.
Some campaigns contain more lies than others.
Some campaigns are about nothing but lies.
Some States have become Red or Blue because of lies.
Some States have become Red or Blue in spite of lies. (17)

There don't seem to be many checks or balances on voters, unless you count not letting children or convicted felons vote, etc. Voters are free to be just as dumb or just as intelligent as they want to be. Voters are free to believe what they want to believe, or decide however they want to decide. Why, they're even free not to vote. When all is said and done, and all the votes are counted, they count them Red or Blue. But the votes of these individuals don't count as much as the votes of the States in the Electoral College. That's where an accumulation of Red States or Blue States determine the election of one candidate or another. Except in 2000 when there were five Red votes and four Blue votes in the U. S. Supreme Court. In that case those were the votes that counted the most. (18)

In this country we have always had Red States and Blue States. That is the nature of the political process. It is a winner-take-all system, where whoever receives the most popular votes in a State wins all that State's electoral votes. It is only recently that the graphical representation of Red and Blue on a map of all the States has come to be used. If it had been used fifty years ago, the Solid South would have been Blue. Today the South is still solid, but it's Red. (19)

Blue States have just as many dumb voters as Red States do. Red States have just as many informed voters as Blue States do. It's just that when Red State voters and Blue State voters think about their choices for President they somehow reach different conclusions and vote accordingly. (20)

Is there something we can identify and say, "This is the essence of a Red State or a Blue State?" In some ways you'd want to say that a Red State is Republican and Conservative, whereas a Blue State is Democratic and Liberal. But these qualities are not absolute. Red States have voted Blue, and Blue States have voted Red, at least historically speaking. Of course there are exceptions. The District of Columbia, it seems, has always voted Democratic or Liberal, and therefore could be essentially Blue. Kansas could be considered essentially Red, as could most of the Great Plains States, despite the fact they voted for Lyndon Johnson in 1964. The Northeastern States are essentially Blue, despite the fact they voted for Nixon and Reagan during their landslide years. But what is the essence of Redness or Blueness? We're still looking. (21)

The sage manifests humility to all the world. In recent years we have heard our politicians speak about humility, but have we seen them manifest it? George W. Bush has been in power now for awhile. Before that it was Clinton of the Blues, Reagan/Bush Red and Carter Blue. You might have to go all the way back to Ford, if even then, to find a humble President, and he wasn't elected to the office. The Presidency is not about humility, although it could be. I don't think a humble man could be elected President. A candidate might say he was humble, like George W. Bush did in 2000, but was he truly humble or was that just rhetoric? It takes a great deal of pride and even some arrogance to run for President, much less to win. In Presidential Politics humble guys finish last. (22)

Do the Red States and Blue States agree on anything? Of course they do. It is difficult to notice any agreement, however, especially during an election year because they are so busy disagreeing with each other. During a non-election year it is the representatives of the Red States and Blue States in Congress who perpetuate the contentious atmosphere.

What are some things that everyone agrees with, or should agree with? They can be found in the Declaration of Independence and the Constitution. (23)

The candidates stood up, with ideas clearly distinguishable from each other, and political parties came forth, Republican and Democratic. From these parties came the ideas of Red and Blue, in the minds of the media, in the minds of the voters, and in the minds of thinkers, political and non-political, trying to make sense of this dichotomy. Where did it come from? Where is it going? Where could it go? How could it be changed? What does it mean for me? What does it mean for the country? So far, there are so many questions, known and unknown, and so few answers. (25)

What goes up will come down, eventually, and in what could be called something like "The Political Law of Gravity," what is Red today could be Blue tomorrow. A politician can never take anything for granted. If he does he runs the risk of becoming an ex-politician. (26)

The men and women behind a President, advising him, telling him what to do, often leave no trace of their advising and telling, but their influence is often just as important as that of the President himself. Their advice can get us into a war or keep us out, for example; and in political campaigns, it is they, by their strategic decisions, who often decide which States become Red or Blue. (27)

Relations between Red States and Blue States can be compared to relations between men and women. In an election, one type of State, Red or Blue, is clearly dominant, whereas the other type of State, the losers, like it or not, must submit to that dominance. Relations between men and women are often struggles for dominance as well. (28)

The Presidency is within anyone's grasp. All you have to do is figure out how to put together the most electoral votes from the Red States or the Blue States. Of course a candidate must choose a color, Red or Blue. He can't be both Red and Blue.

If a candidate wins a State, it becomes his color. A State is not any color really until people vote and the votes are counted. But after the votes are counted, and when the results become clear, the State is designated a particular color, and it remains that color for the next four years. (29)

Making a State turn Red or Blue requires decisive action. Any hesitation, any passivity can cost valuable votes. A candidate and his advisors must be firmly rooted in political reality, which is not necessarily the same as actual reality. (30)

In the political climate of the early twenty-first century it seems that the Red States are more militant than the Blue States. Of course everyone can support a war if it is necessary, but not everyone can support a war if it seems merely expedient, and this is one reason the Blue States now differ with the Red States: some of our recent military action has seemed to be unnecessary. (31)

The relationship of Red States and Blue States to the electoral process is like the relationship of the ocean to all the great rivers and streams which feed into it. And whoever best controls the electoral process, in great measure determines the distribution of Red States and Blue States. (32)

Red States and Blue States
Help us make sense of
And validate
An often chaotic
Capricious
Complicated
Controversial
Election process. (32)

Voters who think
The country is moving
In the wrong direction
Will not always vote for change.
If they did,
There would have been more
Blue States in 2004
Than actually voted that way. (33)

The Red States are always trying to achieve a permanent majority over the Blue States, and vice versa. This is true with regard to the Presidency and both houses of Congress, as well as the Governors' mansions, and State legislatures throughout the country. Such a permanent majority seems unlikely, but if it did happen it would permanently define the character of the United States as perceived by those at home and abroad. It is doubtful whether or not that is a good thing. (34)

Red States and Blue States both seek to be the center of attraction for voters, but in the final analysis one always succeeds better than the other.

And then there is the matter of benevolence: are the winners always benevolent to the losers? Are the losers always benevolent to the winners? The struggle that ends on election night often begins a conflict that continues until the next election. (35)

The Red States and Blue States are not passive entities. They are active in electing a President. The height of their importance occurs on the day when the Electoral College meets to cast and count their votes. After that, they stand as an emblem of the election just held, a symbol which serves to legitimatize the man who was elected President. (37)

Red States and Blue States
Do not always vote
For a candidate
Who is entirely truthful.
Often they vote
For a candidate
Who says what they want to hear.

Some States abide by what is solid.
Some States abide by what is soft.
Some dwell with the fruit.
Some dwell with the flower.
But the choices they make
Have a profound and lasting
Impact on our nation
As a whole,
Not to mention
The whole world. (38)

A man is never satisfied with a majority of votes from the Red States or Blue States. If he has a winning margin, he wants a mandate. If he has a mandate, he wants a landslide. Presidential candidates have egos much larger than the proportion of votes they receive. (38)

When we look at the different parts of a Red State, we do not see what makes those parts add up to become a Red State. The sky is just as blue in a Blue State as it is in a Red State. The grass is just as green in a Red State as it is in a Blue State. But Red States depend on Blue States for their existence. If there were no Blue States, there would be no need for Red States. The color scheme was invented to indicate differences, not similarities. Yet wherever you look, similarities are all you see. It's too bad the people living there often can't find more common ground for agreement. (39)

It has been said there's not a dime's worth of difference between the two major political parties, the Republicans and the Democrats, the Reds and the Blues. But that's not true. There is more than a dime's worth of difference. In fact, in many ways, the Reds are really opposite from the Blues.

The Republican mind is different from the Democratic mind. It is not genetic, or anything like that, but Republicans just believe different things, and think in different ways than Democrats do. This becomes obvious when you listen to the two sides debate a topic of social importance; also when you listen to pundits from opposing sides give their spins on things. (That is, if you can listen to the spin without becoming ill.) There may not be a dime's worth of difference between politicians and spinmeisters, of whatever ilk, but positions taken by opposing parties on important issues often could not be more distinct from each other. (40)

The United States
Is United
In spite of,
Or perhaps because of
Red States
And Blue States. (41)

One nation produces one election.
One election produces two, Red and Blue.
Red and Blue produce
One winner
One President
One nation
Which adds up to
One. (42)

The battle for supremacy in Red States and Blue States is not for the meek or the soft. It is for bold and tenacious fighters. The boldest and most tenacious stands the best chance of winning in a contest where winning is everything, and where the outcome will have an impact on the course of history. Therefore one should not minimize the process which results in a State's becoming Red or Blue. (43)

Red or Blue?
Which is the most precious
For our nation and her people—
All her people?
This is a question
That is rarely,
If ever answered
On election night. (44)

Reds act on things that Blues regard as unnecessary.
Blues act on things that Reds regard as unnecessary.
In the exercise of our Government,
Depending on which side is in power,
And to what degree that power exists,
Someone always gets to complain
That their needs and wants
Are not being met. (45)

Thomas Jefferson said we have a right to the Pursuit of Happiness.
But some people are happy when the Reds are in power,
And some are happy when the Blues are in power.
Under our political system it seems that
You can't make all the people happy all the time. (46)

It is easier to vote in some States than in others.
It is easier to get it right in some States than in others.
It is easier to count all the votes in some States than in others.
It is easier to make your vote count in some States than in others. (47)

The more information some people have, the more inclined they are to vote for a particular candidate. The more information other people have, or think they have, the more inclined they are to vote against a candidate. Politicians know this about voters. That is why they sometimes run negative campaigns. If they can't get you to vote for their man, maybe they can get you to vote against his opponent. So the distribution of Red States and Blue States often reflects something negative rather than something positive. (48)

A man does not run for President by himself,
And he is as good or as bad
As those who are helping him.
A bad candidate can be helped to win,
And a good candidate can be helped to lose.
In the end it all depends
On how his message is received
In the Red States and Blue States. (49)

It is sometimes more important for a candidate to display a winning attitude than for him to talk about the issues. This is one of the paradoxes of Politics. A State can sometimes be influenced to vote Red or Blue by factors having nothing to do with logic or truth, right or wrong. (50)

Red States and Blue States don't really exist until everyone has voted and the votes have been counted. The States are then assigned a color based upon the outcome of the vote.

It would not be incorrect to say that the concepts of Red States and Blue States mean nothing and they mean a lot. Before the polls close on election day, color is potential only. After the polls close, and until the next election, the colors have their meaning, of which everyone has his own understanding and interpretation. (51)

When you're in a Red State you might think you know what kind of people you'll meet, just as when you're in a Blue State you have a preconception of what kind of people live there. And some of the stereotypes are correct. There are lots of rowdy rednecks and brusque New Yorkers, for example. But the main thing you find, if travel from State to State, Red or Blue, is that the people who live there are not that much different from me and you. (52)

The word *Tao* means "Way." This is an important concept in Politics. For example, there is a Red State Way, with all that encompasses, and a Blue State Way, equally complex. We could ponder these concepts for a long time and probably never fully explain them. And their meaning changes according to who the candidate is. The Red Way of George W. Bush is different from that of George H. W. Bush. The Blue Way of John Kerry is different from that of Al Gore. The flexibility that each Way possesses is one of its greatest sources of power. (53)

If our country were a garden
Planted here with
Red flowers,
There with Blue,
Then every four years
The flowers are dug up
And the garden
Is planted anew.
They are watered
And nourished
By a long campaign.
Then on election night
And on succeeding days
The flowers come out
In full bloom. (54)

People who were born in Red States rarely move to Blue States. But many people who were born in Blue States seem to be migrating to Red States in droves. Ask most any Southerner, for example, and he can attest to the fact that things are noticeably different "since all those Yankees came down here." Needless to say they're not overjoyed about all that. But the Northerners are not always that happy either. They sometimes don't fit into their new surroundings and have trouble feeling really at home, spiritually or politically. But if enough people from Blue States move to Red States, that might turn a Red State into a Blue State. The transplanted Northerners might be happier then. (55)

There is something noble about a President, but there are many things about Presidential candidates that are not noble. In order to win a Red State or a Blue State, a person must engage in Politics, and Politics can be really unsavory. If the path to the White House was all about serving the Red States and Blue States then it might be different. A Presidential campaign might be nobler. But it is also about power, and as we know power corrupts, hence the lack of nobility often displayed in running for President. (56)

Can a Red President be elected from a Blue State, or a Blue President be elected from a Red State? I'm sure both Rudolf Giuliani (R) of New York and John Edwards (D) of North Carolina have thought about these questions as the 2008 election approaches. Of course any candidate can be elected from anywhere. Ronald Reagan came from California, which has recently been a solid Blue State, and Bill Clinton came from Arkansas, which is essentially a Red State. But since the last eleven elections have been won by candidates from the Southern half of the country, geography may be an important factor in determining our next President. Maybe Giuliani and Edwards will think about that as well. (57)

In some Blue States there is a Red State hiding just beneath the surface, waiting to be brought out. Given a few different votes here or there, the result itself would be different. The same is true of Red States, just not as many of them. The Red States seem to be more firmly Red, whereas some of the Blue States seem to be more up for grabs. For example, I can't imagine Kansas going Blue, but I can imagine California going Red. In fact, California was Red in every election from 1968 through 1988. A State, therefore, is usually one color or the other only in retrospect, not looking forward. (58)

In order to know what kind of plant you have, it is sufficient to examine its seeds or roots. Oak trees grow from acorns. The roots of a daffodil don't resemble those of a rose.

In order to know what color a State will be, one can examine its political roots. They are sometimes just as unambiguous as are those of a flower. But sometimes they're not, and that's why we have the election. (59)

Winning the Red States and Blue States
Is like eating a small fish:
You want to eat all the meat
And leave the bones for your opponent. (60)

In putting together
A majority of votes
From Red States or Blue States
Sometimes a small State
Is just as important as
A large State.
Ask Al Gore, 2000. (61)

A Blue State is not bad because it votes for the loser in an election, and a Red State is not good because it votes for the winner. Voting is one of our fundamental rights. Simply exercising that right is good, and in some ways not exercising it is not good, although everyone is free to vote for anyone they choose, or not to vote at all. At the end, when all the votes are tallied, and the results are known, the losers may say the outcome was bad and the winners may say it was good, but history will have the final say. (62)

An electoral majority begins with a small core of Red States or Blue States, then grows as more people make up their minds, decide to vote or not to vote, whatever. Many factors go into determining the outcome of an election, even the weather. But thank God that when it rains, it falls on Republicans and Democrats equally. (63)

The election of
A President
Begins with a single vote.
The election map
Of Red and Blue
Begins with a single State. (64)

Do Red State people
Dislike Blue State candidates?
Do Blue State people
Distrust Red State candidates? (65)

When the Red States dominate, the Blue States have the blues.
When the Blue States prevail, the Red States see red.
It is difficult to have a happy nation
When half its citizens are disgruntled. (66)

Between the Red States and Blue States
There are three precious things:
Cooperation
Compromise
Consensus.

Too often we find
Conflict
Contrariety
Contention. (67)

A Presidential campaign is like a war, and the electoral map of Red and Blue is like a map of the battlefield, of territory won and lost. Even some martial terminology is used, as when we talk about battleground states, etc. But a campaign is not a war. No shots are fired; no lives are lost. The whole process is entirely peaceful, as one might expect from a nation of laws. And no blood is shed, only tears of joy and disappointment. (68)

Much of the *Tao Te Ching* uses ideas that seem strange to Americans. For exam-ple, "I do not dare advance an inch; I prefer to retreat a foot." How many people would agree with that? Not many, I'm sure, and certainly not many American politicians. (69)

Sometimes it seems
That a State
Is more easily swayed
Red or Blue
By a lie
Than by what's true. (70)

No one,
From any State,
Red or Blue,
Has a monopoly
On what's false
And what's true. (71)

Do more
Thinking, caring,
Inquiring voters
Live in Red States
Or in Blue States? (72)

A Presidential candidate
Is like a fisherman
Who casts his nets
Into the sea
And hauls in States—
Large or small,
Populous or not,
Red or Blue—
Then hoists them
Onto the scales
To weigh his catch
Against the other side.

The winner has his photo snapped,
Posing with his prize.
The loser gets to grouse
About the one that got away. (73)

Everyone is more fearful now than they were before 9/11. Fear can influence elections, sometimes tipping a State from one color to another. Politicians know this, and they play on these fears. Sometimes the outcome of an election hinges on which candidate gets out the clearest message of fear. (74)

Many questions dealing with taxes tend to separate Red State voters from Blue State voters. It would be nice if these issues could bring people together instead of driving them apart. (75)

We've all heard the philosophical conundrum: If a tree falls in the forest, with no one around to hear it, does it make a sound?

If the people have spoken, but no one was listening, did they say anything?

If a person votes Blue, and his State becomes Red, does his Blue vote count? How? Where?

If 51 million people vote Blue, and 50 million people vote Red, what does it mean if Red wins? (76)

We hear much discussion in the news of surpluses and deficits, and it's good that we do, but in many instances they are just talking about numbers. The surpluses and deficits that are the most important are the ones that are the most difficult to quantify. It would be nice if we had a surplus in Washington of honesty, altruism, virtue, amity, justice, and respect for the law. Outside Washington it would be nice if we had a surplus of good will between the Red States and the Blue States. (77)

The Blues were in control of the White House for eight years during the 1990s. Did they look for ways to include the Reds in the national dialogue?

The Reds are in control of the White House now. Are the Blues being included or excluded?

Does either side really care about what the other side thinks? Or are they so focused on building majorities and pursuing agendas that consensus is ignored? Majorities may come and go, but consensus has a way of healing. (78)

The Red States and Blue States should seek to reconcile with each other as soon after an election as possible. But this sort of harmony is not always sought and rarely achieved.

It would be better for our leaders to hold fast to the needs of our nation as a whole than to focus too much on the needs of the Red States or the Blue States. (79)

The graphical representation of Red States and Blue States illustrates (but often exaggerates) the size of a Red State majority, which in terms of actual votes cast may be quite small, or even nonexistent, but in terms of geographical area looks quite large. (80)

What is the Way of
Victory? Is it
The Red State Way
Or the Blue State Way?
This is a question
That must be answered
Every four years. (81)

Epilogue

Here are two websites that the reader might find interesting and edifying:

http://answers.google.com/answers/threadview?id=415905

http://en.wikipedia.org/wiki/Red_state_vs._blue_state_divide

There may be other references via Google or other search engines. One good thing about the Internet and other research tools is that you never know what you'll find until you start looking.

978-0-595-35967-7
0-595-35967-1